Communicate Across Cultures

Cultures

Unlocking the Secrets of
Intercultural Communication

Table of Contents

Chapter 1. Introduction

Dive into an enriching exploration of diversity with our Special Report: "Communicate Across Cultures: Unlocking the Secrets of Intercultural Communication". This fascinating journey does not take you through complex algorithms or abstract theories, but through the colorful tapestry of global cultures and languages. Enlighten yourself about the intricacies of human interaction, untangling misunderstandings and fostering unity. Our world is a symphony of cultures, and your ability to connect and empathize across cultural boundaries could be the harmonious note you contribute. Whether you're a jet-setting entrepreneur or a curious soul thirsty for knowledge, this report is designed to captivate your interest and supplement your interpersonal skills. With a seemingly simple purchase, you'll be embarking on a journey that can transform how you connect with the world. So why wait? Buy our comprehensive report today - it's time you unlocked the secrets of Intercultural Communication.

Chapter 2. The Art of Intercultural Communication: An Overview

Intercultural communication refers to the complex process through which individuals from different cultural backgrounds endeavor to exchange thoughts, ideas, and meanings. It involves verbal, nonverbal, and implicit forms of communication, all influenced by various cultural norms, values, traditions, and societal contexts. Understanding these dynamics is crucial given the interconnectedness of our global community.

2.1. Foundations of Intercultural Communication

How we perceive and engage with other cultures initially relies on our construct of culture itself. Culture shapes our values, trends, traditions, and behaviors, defining what we deem "normal" or "acceptable." However, these are not universal norms; they vary from one society to another. This inherent diversity fosters a rich world, yet it also presents challenges when communicating across cultures. A gesture considered polite in one culture might be offensive in another, a phrase acceptable in one language might not translate well into another. Therefore, understanding cultural backgrounds is fundamental to successful intercultural communication.

2.2. The Role of Language

Language is the primary tool of communication, carrying cultures' beliefs, values, and worldviews. It's not just about words and syntax, it embodies the way people think, reason, and see the world. When engaging in intercultural communication, recognizing subtle nuances in language can prevent misunderstandings. Bilinguals and multilinguals often report feeling different when speaking different languages, signifying different cultural modes of thought in action.

2.3. The Importance of Nonverbal Communication

Just as with verbal communication, nonverbal cues also deeply influence cross-cultural conversations. Facial expressions, hand gestures, personal space—these all contribute to communication and carry cultural codes. For instance, while direct eye contact is considered respectful in Western societies, it can be interpreted as disrespectful in some Asian cultures. Recognizing and respecting these nonverbal differences is vital in intercultural communication.

2.4. Developing Intercultural Competency

Acquiring intercultural competency starts with enhancing cultural self-awareness—understanding one's own cultural values, beliefs, biases, and assumptions. With that foundation, the next step is learning about other cultures: their history, traditions, values, and language. This awareness kindles empathy, allowing for more effective communication and cooperation.

2.5. The Impact of Stereotypes and Prejudices

Stereotypes and prejudices create barriers in intercultural interaction, causing miscommunication and potential conflict. These often stem from a lack of understanding or misinformation that prompts negative assumptions about another culture. Unlearning these biases and working towards unbiased, respectful cultural interaction can greatly improve intercultural communication.

2.6. Intercultural Communication in a Globalized World

With globalization, the need for effective intercultural communication has grown exponentially. As we come into daily contact with a diverse range of cultures, both physically and virtually, cultural understanding has become more critical than ever. Companies, for instance, must recognize cultural differences to build strong relationships with international partners, while educators need to adapt their teaching methods for culturally diverse classrooms.

2.7. Bridging Cultural Gaps

Bridging cultural gaps starts with recognizing and respecting cultural differences. Active listening, open dialogue, and empathy are key to overcoming these cultural barriers. When in doubt, asking polite, respectful questions can facilitate understanding. Remember, the goal of intercultural communication isn't to make everyone the same; instead, it's about creating mutual understanding and harmony amidst diversity.

2.8. Encountering Challenges in Intercultural Communication

Even with the best intentions and preparation, challenges in intercultural communication persist. Misunderstandings can occur due to language problems, cultural differences, or simple misinterpretation. Yet, these challenges can become opportunities for learning with the right mindset. Adopting an attitude of curiosity and patience can pave the way for greater understanding and connection.

2.9. Building a More Inclusive World through Intercultural Communication

At its heart, intercultural communication is about building bridges. It fosters understanding, respect, and acceptance of diverse cultures. By enhancing our intercultural communication skills, we can contribute to a more inclusive, understanding, and effectively interconnected world. This, in the end, is the essence and the art of intercultural communication.

This chapter is a mere introduction and insight into the complex and fascinating world of intercultural communication. The following chapters will delve deeper into these subjects, offering practical strategies to improve one's intercultural communication skills and better navigate our diverse world.

Chapter 3. Decoding Non-Verbal Language Across Cultures

The understanding of non-verbal communication plays a pivotal role in intercultural communication. It is a silent orchestra orchestrating our verbal language, often communicating more about our emotions, attitudes, and thoughts than words themselves. However, interpreting these non-verbal cues across cultures can be a challenging task as they often bear different connotations and meanings based on cultural context.

3.1. Non-Verbal Language: An Overview

Non-verbal communication constitutes all forms of expression that do not use words, including body language, facial expressions, eye contact, gestures, touch, posture, spatial relationships, as well as other non-vocal and non-linguistic elements such as timing, tone, and intensity of voice, and dressing style. Studies show that non-verbal behaviours make up a significant portion of our daily interpersonal communication, making it crucial for cross-cultural understanding.

Key considerations for decoding non-verbal cues in cross-cultural communication involve knowledge of how different cultures perceive and utilize them, as well as the speaker and listener's level of comfort with them.

3.2. The Role of Body Language

Body language is a powerful form of non-verbal communication used universally but interpreted differently across cultures. It covers a broad spectrum of attributes, including posture, movements, and gestures. For example, the handshake, a standard greeting in many western countries, might not be appropriate in some Asian cultures where it can be viewed as invasive. A simple nod might signify agreement in one culture, while in others, it may be a show of respect.

Reading body language across cultures requires a nuanced understanding of the cultural context and history of the individuals involved. It is fundamental for effective cross-cultural communication to avoid misinterpretations that could lead to miscommunications and misunderstandings.

3.3. Facial Expressions and Eye Contact

Facial expressions, particularly those conveying basic emotions, are generally considered universal. Research agrees that smiles, frowns, and expressions of fear, surprise, disgust, and happiness are understood worldwide. However, the intensity, appropriateness, and frequency of these expressions can vary significantly across cultures.

Eye contact also carries different meanings across cultures. In several Western cultures, making and maintaining eye contact is considered a sign of honesty and trustworthiness, whereas, in some Asian and African cultures, sustained eye contact may be seen as disrespectful or aggressive.

3.4. Gestures and Their Cultural Implications

Gestures are another vital aspect of non-verbal communication. They include movements and signs made by our hands, arms, head, and even legs. The thumbs-up sign illustrates well the varying cultural interpretations of gestures: in most Western cultures, it denotes approval or agreement; in Middle Eastern cultures, it may be considered offensive.

The list of such culturally specific differences is extensive, highlighting the crucial need for careful research and understanding when navigating through cultural exchanges.

3.5. Role of Personal Space

The utilization of personal space is also a significant, although often overlooked, component of non-verbal communication. Known as proxemics, it studies how individuals use space to communicate. This involves not only physical distance between individuals (personal or interpersonal space) but also the space within social and public contexts.

Personal space can dramatically vary between cultures. In North American and Northern European countries, considerable distance is often maintained as a sign of respect for personal space, while in Latin American or Middle Eastern cultures, closeness is a sign of friendliness and warmness.

To function effectively in an intercultural environment, it's vital to recognize these variations and respect the personal space expectations of counterparts from different backgrounds.

3.6. The Significance of Paralanguage

Paralanguage involves all aspects of the voice that aren't actual words—variations in pitch, volume, speed, and tone, or use of sounds like "uh-huh", "hmm", and so on. The meanings and importance of these vocal nuances can significantly vary between cultures, so understanding them can be very insightful.

3.7. Dressing Style as Non-Verbal Communication

One's attire communicates a substantial amount about who they are, their social class, occupation, or ethnicity, often revealing many unspoken cultural norms and principles.

3.8. Deciphering Silence

Silence, an essential aspect of non-verbal communication, often bears culture-specific interpretations. For instance, in many Western cultures, silence may denote awkwardness or signify that someone has nothing to contribute, while in Eastern cultures, silence is seen as a sign of respect and thoughtful communication.

In conclusion, decoding non-verbal language across cultures is an intricate task requiring an understanding of not just the alien culture, but also the fact that people within the same culture can express non-verbals differently. Intercultural proficiency is not simply about understanding foreign languages or traditions—it's about appreciating, adapting, and reciprocating the intricate layers of non-verbal communication that enrich our global tapestry. By increasing our understanding and sensitivity to these non-verbal cues, we can bridge cultural gaps, improving communication, unity, and understanding across cultures.

Chapter 4. The Role of Language: Understanding Verbal Communication

Language, beyond its quintessential role as a system of communication, serves as the very bedrock of culture and perception. It is not just a string of words or sounds; it's a powerful tool that shapes our reality and helps us understand the world.

4.1. Function of Language in Communication

Language is the primary means by which we communicate our thoughts, intentions, and emotions with those around us. By transforming intangible thoughts into concrete verbal expressions we can share our subjective experiences with others.

The usefulness of language extends beyond individual interactions to forming collective norms, laws, and societal structures. Indeed, language has helped shape human civilizations from the dawn of time, enabling shared understanding, cooperation, and collective progress.

4.2. Language Diversity: Reflecting Cultural Diversity

Language diversity is a testament to human cultural diversity. Today, we can count approximately 7,000 active languages in the world. Each of these languages is unique, reflecting the cultural richness of the communities it serves.

Languages are not merely collections of words. They carry the weight of the culture, history, and values of the communities that speak them. Moreover, they play an integral part in shaping the thought process of those communities. Different languages can significantly impact how individuals perceive the world, highlighting the substantive links between language, culture and thought.

4.3. Semantics: The Meanings Behind Words

Semantics, a branch of linguistics, studies the meanings of words and sentences. Each language has its own semantic system, which can present challenges during intercultural communication.

Literal translation from one language to another can sometimes alter the original meaning or even render the translation nonsensical. Understanding the semantics of a language imparts not only the meaning of the words itself but also the intended message, which may often be implicit.

4.4. The Power of Context in Language

In using language to communicate, context is pivotal. Whether it is spoken or written, language relies heavily on situational context, which includes the speaker's and listener's relationships, the situation, culture, and even the medium of communication. For instance, the phrase "I'm fine," can have polar opposite meanings based on the speaker's tone and context.

Moreover, high and low context cultures differ in their reliance on explicit verbal communication. High context cultures, like many Asian societies, heavily rely on non-verbal cues and implicit communication, often embedding much of the message in the context. On the other end, low context cultures, like many Western societies, rely more on explicit verbal communication.

4.5. Non-Verbal Communication: Complementing Language

The importance of non-verbal cues in communication cannot be underestimated. Body language, facial expressions, gestures, spacing, and even silence play a significant role in conveying messages and emotions.

Non-verbal communication can complement, reinforce, substitute, or contradict verbal communication. For instance, when a person's words are contradicted by their body language, others are more likely to believe the non-verbal message.

4.6. Language as a Reflection of Societal Norms and Values

Language mirrors societal values and norms. Its rhythm, phrases, and words, all reflect aspects of a society's culture — from how people view time to how they relate to nature, authority, individuality, and collectivity.

4.7. Learning a New Language: Delving into a New Culture

Learning a new language is not just about expanding communication capacity; it is a plunge into a new culture. It enhances intercultural understanding and empathy, allowing learners to see the world from the perspective of a different cultural group.

4.8. Conclusion

Language goes beyond mere verbal exchange. It is a cultural identifier, a tool for social navigation, and a carrier of values, norms, and perceptions. The vast diversity of languages complicate intercultural communication, and yet on many levels, they also enrich it, enabling glimpses into different worldviews and perspectives. Understanding language's cultural ties can bridge gaps, reduce misunderstandings, and foster more effective, positive communication across cultures.

Chapter 5. Cultural Nuances: The Power and Importance of Context

Understanding the cultural context is vital for effective communication across different cultures. It not only involves interpreting the messages sent by other people, but also needs a deep realization of the set of rules, norms, and conventions based on people's location, religion, social structure, and even personal experiences. This is the complex underpinning that we are unraveling in this chapter, where we explore the power and relevance of context in varied cultures.

5.1. The Contextual Spectrum: High-Context and Low-Context Cultures

Anthropologist Edward T. Hall was instrumental in identifying two types of societies based on how they communicate: high-context and low-context cultures. High-context cultures mostly rely on implicit communication, where most of the information resides in the physical context or internalized in the person. These cultures often use non-verbal cues, which necessitates a deep understanding and familiarity with the culture to interpret the messages correctly. Japan, China, and Arabic cultures are classic examples of high-context societies, where the communication goes beyond the literal words.

On the other end of the spectrum, we have the low-context cultures where communication is explicit. Messages are conveyed clearly, and extra emphasis is placed on precision and clarity with verbal expression. Most Western cultures, including the U.S., Canada, and Germany, fall into this category.

Understanding this distinction is critical, as communicating across these cultural divides without an awareness of these nuances can lead to grave misunderstandings.

5.2. The Role of Silence in High-Context Cultures

In high-context cultures, the power of silence is immense and often signifies a level of respect, agreement, or contemplation. Japan, a high-context society, recognizes the concept of 'Ma,' which pertains to the vital spaces or pauses between actions. Rather than being an empty void, 'Ma' is full of potential. It represents a pause for reflection, a moment to fully understand, and an opportunity to absorb information. In contrast, in low-context cultures like the U.S., silence is often uncomfortable and equated with awkwardness or disengagement. Recognizing the meaning of silence in different cultures can pave the way for more accurate and successful intercultural communication.

5.3. Divergent Interpretations of Eye Contact

Eye contact, another powerful non-verbal cue, varies in its interpretation across cultures. In Western societies, consistent eye contact is regarded as a sign of attentiveness and respect. However, the same act is considered rude and intrusive in many Asian cultures. For example, in a Japanese interpersonal conversation, speakers may avoid direct eye contact as a way to respect the listener's personal space.

5.4. Understanding Power Distance in Cultural Contexts

The concept of Power Distance, a term coined by sociologist Geert Hofstede, is another crucial aspect to consider for intercultural communication. It defines the extent to which the less powerful members of institutions and organizations within a country expect and accept that power is distributed unequally. Cultures with high power-distance, such as Malaysia, Guatemala, and the Philippines, are hierarchical, with clear distinctions between superiors and subordinates. On the other hand, low power-distance societies like Denmark, Netherlands, and Austria favor flatter organizations and shared decision-making.

5.5. Relationship Orientation: Collectivism vs Individualism

Intercultural communication also requires an understanding of a culture's relationship orientation. Some cultures prioritize communal relationships and group identity, known as collectivism, like many Asian and African cultures. In contrast, western cultures often promote individual liberties and personal achievements, defining an individualistic culture. These orientations greatly shape communication, from negotiation tactics to conflict resolution, and even expressions of agreement or disagreement.

This chapter has unpacked the intricate layers of cultural nuances and the vast significance of context in intercultural communication. A deep-seated understanding of these aspects will facilitate successful communication across cultures, fostering a unity among an incredible diversity. It acts as a mirror, reflecting the enormous heterogeneity of our world and the ways to productively interact within it. The power and importance of context in communication cannot be overstressed, emphasizing that communicating across cultures is as much about understanding the unspoken as it is about mastering the language.

Chapter 6. Harnessing Empathy for Effective Cross-Cultural Connection

Emphasizing empathy is the cornerstone to establishing effective cross-cultural connections. Today's globalized community necessitates communication and coordination among diverse groups of people. In a world multilayered with various cultures, beliefs, and customs, empathy is the glue that forges understanding and mutual respect. We must not only comprehend the language and customs of our international companions but also empathize with their individual perspectives.

6.1. Understanding Empathy

Empathy is defined as the ability to comprehend, share, and respond adequately to the feelings of others. This profound sharing of experiences allows for the creation of a bridging space- the empathy gap- between individuals of differing backgrounds and cultures. When we exercise empathy, we build more profound connections and nurture stronger relationships, which aids in the smooth navigation through the mazes of cross-cultural complexities.

To genuinely empathize with someone, we need to possess both a cognitive and emotional understanding. Cognitive empathy involves perspective taking, the intellectual capacity to recognize and comprehend another individual's mental state. Emotional empathy, on the other hand, is the capacity to emotionally respond to another person's mental state.

Integration of these two types of empathy enhances our capacity to form fully effective and all-encompassing empathetic attitudes, enabling us to better navigate cross-cultural communication scenarios.

6.2. The Role of Empathy in Cross-cultural Communication

In cross-cultural communication, exercising empathy isn't optional—it's fundamental. It's an enabling tool for connection, facilitating better understanding and alleviation of inherent biases and stereotypes. Without empathy, cultural differences can drown shared objectives and result in misunderstandings, conflicts, and disjunctions.

Effective communication, whether in a professional or social environment, often relies upon empathetic understanding. To truly hear what another person is saying—without judgment or residual bias—and to respond with understanding, is vital.

Empathy allows for connection despite cultural disparity, encouraging positive interactions, fostering peace, and contributing to global stability. Therefore, harnessing empathy directly links to creating cross-cultural harmony.

6.3. Ways to Harness Empathy for Effective Cross-Cultural Communication

Cultivating empathy isn't a spontaneous process but rather requires regular practice and conscious effort. Consider the following strategies for fostering your empathetic abilities.

6.4. Cultivating Empathy: Practical Steps

Lastly, taking the initiative: If we want to understand others, we must first show a strong desire to know about their customs, values and beliefs. By taking the initiative to learn about other cultures, we can bridge the gap that prevents empathy.

Building empathetic prowess demands practice, exposure, and a solid understanding of its importance. Below, you'll find concrete steps you can take to nourish your empathetic abilities.

6.5. The Payoff of Empathy in Cross-Cultural Connections

Reflect: Reflecting upon your actions and communications can further foster empathy. Reflect on whether you're really hearing others, understanding their points of view, or empathizing with their feelings.

Upon mastering empathy, the benefits reaped are multifold. Better communication results in smoother collaboration, which is advantageous in both professional and personal endeavors. This also reduces room for misunderstandings, hostility, and conflicts, thereby promoting peace and harmony.

Empathy fosters mutual respect, understanding, and appreciation, overcoming the barriers created by cultural diversity. It bridges gaps, unites people, and allows for the exchange of ideas and values. The payoffs are twofold: Not only does it enrich us personally, but it also promotes global harmony—a salient feature of today's interconnected world.

6.6. Conclusion

In essence, empathy is the cornerstone of effective cross-cultural communication. By fostering empathetic understanding, we can step over language and cultural barriers to forge a connection on a more profound, human level. With Practice, patience, and understanding, all of us can harness the power of empathy and employ it to build a seamless bridge uniting cultures worldwide.

Chapter 7. Navigating Social Norms Across Different Geographies

Social norms, determined by the shared beliefs and common practices of a community, are key indicators of an area's culture and significantly shape its interactions and transactions. Depending on the region, these can vary greatly, leading to misunderstandings and unintended offenses when left unrecognized. But fret not, for understanding and acknowledging these norms is a skill that can be learned and mastered, enabling you to efficiently navigate through diverse social landscapes.

7.1. Understanding Social Norms

Social norms serve as a guideline for acceptable behavior within a culture and are usually conditioned by traditions, religion, historical events, and even geography. They consist of both implicit rules, which aren't openly discussed but are understood within the community, and explicit rules, which are formally stated and communicated. They influence myriad aspects of life, including comportment, etiquette, respect for authority, punctuality, and attire. By familiarizing ourselves with these norms, we can foster cultural sensitivity and improve communication by avoiding misunderstandings due to cultural variances.

7.2. Western and Eastern Norms

When addressing the term 'west', it usually refers to European and North American cultures, whereas the 'east' denotes Asia. Western cultures are often described as individualistic societies where a person's needs and rights are prioritized over the group's needs, whereas Eastern cultures are collectivistic, prioritizing harmony, community, and family over individual desires.

In Western cultures, direct communication is the norm and is seen as a sign of honesty and respect. On the contrary, Eastern cultures often engage in indirect communication to avoid conflict and to maintain dignity and face for oneself and for others. Attire conventions also vary significantly; Western cultures are generally more liberal, while Eastern cultures tend to be conservative due to religious influences.

7.3. Navigating Across Asian Contexts

Asia, being the largest continent, is marked by an enormous diversity in cultures and social norms. Generally, Asian societies value modesty, harmony, and respect for authority.

In India, for instance, punctuality is important for professional meetings, but social events often start later than the scheduled time. The Japanese, however, value punctuality for all events, viewing lateness as disrespectful. In China, the concept of 'face' or preserving dignity is crucial in every aspect of life. To avoid causing someone 'to lose face', it's essential to express disagreement or negative feedback in a subtle manner, avoiding direct confrontations.

Remember that these are broad strokes, as cultural norms can diverge considerably within each country.

7.4. Navigating Across European Contexts

Europe, a cultural melting pot, presents its unique set of social norms. For instance, Southern Europeans are generally more animated and expressive than those in Northern Europe who are known for their reserve.

In Germany, punctuality is highly appreciated and reflects reliability. Swedes value egalitarianism, hence the Swedish term 'lagom' which means 'just enough' illustrates their preference for moderation and equality. French people place importance on formal etiquette, even in casual social environments.

These nuances are important to remember, informing our behavior while interacting with Europeans.

7.5. Navigating Across American and Australian Contexts

North Americans, particularly the US populace, value independence, directness, and personal space. Australian culture upholds honesty, straightforwardness, and "mateship", a form of camaraderie that emphasizes equality, loyalty, and mutual respect.

Remember, these social norms are not fixed, but are constantly evolving and being redefined by societal changes, technological innovations, and global influences.

7.6. Conclusion

Relying on the norms of one's own culture could lead to a cross-cultural faux pas. As we traverse the world, understanding and respecting local social norms becomes an integral part of our journey. Awareness of these norms equips us not only to participate in diverse cultures but also to create an inclusive environment for others. The world is a vibrant and varied canvas of social norms, and part of the thrill is learning to appreciate its beautiful tapestry.

Always recall that the purpose of this exploration is not to stereotype cultures, but to build competency in cross-cultural communication.

Embrace the norms of other cultures as you would invite others to acknowledge yours. This knowledge is not merely power, but a bridge to profound connections and shared understanding across cultures.

Chapter 8. Attitudes and Beliefs: The Core Pillars of Cultures

Many of the difficulties we encounter when interacting across cultures stem from differences in fundamental attitudes and beliefs. These elements often guide people's perceptions, values, and actions, shaping the societies they belong to. Exploring and understanding these core pillars can therefore greatly enhance cross-cultural communication.

To appreciate attitudes and beliefs' impact on cultures, we should first define these terms. In the realm of psychology, attitudes are defined as evaluations or learned tendencies, guiding us to respond favorably or unfavorably towards certain ideas, objects, or people. Beliefs, on the other hand, refer to convictions or acceptances that certain things are true or exist.

8.1. Understanding the Underpinnings of Attitudes and Beliefs

Attitudes and beliefs originate from a combination of hereditary factors, personal experiences, and cultural contexts. Although hereditary factors and personal experiences are unique to each person, cultural context is shared among a group of people and significantly influences attitudes and beliefs.

These cultural paradigms, which we'll consider as sets of attitudes and beliefs, are often stable and self-reinforcing. For instance, members of a collectivist society may hold beliefs valuing the needs of the group over the individual. Acts reinforcing this belief, such as sharing resources or sacrificing personal achievements for the group's betterment, are then rewarded, reinforcing the belief.

8.2. Attitudes, Beliefs, and Communication

Attitudes and beliefs bear significant weight in intercultural communication. Understanding the attitudes and beliefs unique to a culture helps explain why people from different cultures behave differently in similar situations. It can also pave the way for anticipating how others might react to our behaviors and communications.

For instance, an individual from a culture that values respect for elders may find it challenging to communicate with someone from a relatively egalitarian culture, where all individuals, regardless of their age, are treated equally.

Understanding such attitude-related differences can help bridge cultural divides, influence our communication style, choice of words, gestures, or the manner we show respect or disagreement.

8.3. Role of Attitudes and Beliefs in Forming Cultural Identity

Cultural identity is a critical aspect of an individual's self-concept and overall identity. It influences how individuals perceive themselves and how they relate to the world. Some theories in social psychology propose that attitudes and beliefs contribute significantly to the formation of these identities.

Individuals within a culture often share a common set of attitudes and beliefs. Consequently, these shared elements become identifiers of that particular culture, further reinforcing cultural cohesion and a sense of belonging among members.

8.4. Bridging Cultures Through Understanding Attitudes and Beliefs

Understanding attitudes and beliefs can be a stepping stone towards developing cultural sensitivity and competency. Culturally sensitive individuals can navigate different cultural contexts with ease, build mutual understanding, and demonstrate respect for different cultures.

This process begins with acknowledging cultural diversity and continues with understanding and empathizing with others' attitudes and beliefs. For example, someone raised within a predominantly individualist culture could comprehend the collectivist attitudes of another culture, thereby fostering openness and mutual understanding.

8.5. Conclusion

Examining and understanding attitudes and beliefs is central to fostering effective intercultural communication. By uncovering these core pillars of culture, we increase our ability to understand, connect with, and respect others, regardless of cultural differences.

Remember, understanding these attitudes and beliefs also doesn't entail subduing one's viewpoints. Instead, it is about developing empathy, acknowledging cultural differences, and striving to find common ground. Patience, open-mindedness, and empathy can lead us down rewarding paths of meaningful cross-cultural interactions and universal harmony.

Chapter 9. Conflict and Misunderstanding: The Role of Assumptions in Intercultural Communication

Effective communication between different cultures is complicated by a host of factors, one of the most prominent being assumptions. Assumptions stand tall and formidable - quite crucial, yet dangerous in their potential to set off a storm of misunderstandings and conflicts. They are the bridge between what we perceive and how we interpret it.

9.1. The Anatomy of an Assumption

An assumption is a conclusion, a deduction, or a belief that is accepted as true without proof. Often, it is based on past experiences, cultural norms, personal biases, and stereotypes. It acts as a cognitive shortcut, sparing us the mental labor of thorough thought and rendering swift judgment.

However, these cognitive shortcuts can do more harm than good in intercultural interactions. The complexities of language, non-verbal cues, and social customs make the interpretation of foreign behavior particularly tricky.

In comparison to navigating within our familiar culture, it's akin to reading a book in a foreign language — one might understand the letters, even the words, but the nuances and idioms delicately woven into the narrative may easily elude us. This is where assumptions slip in, filling in the gaps in our comprehension and constructing a narrative to ease our uncertainty.

9.2. The Playground of Assumptions: Stereotypes and Preconceptions

A profound understanding of the diverse cultural expressions necessitates unraveling the elements of stereotypes and preconceptions. More often than not, stereotypes represent an oversimplified, generalized view of a culture, often rooted in limited experiences or third-party narratives. Preconceptions, another common form of assumption, are beliefs or ideas formed in advance, typically before having enough evidence or firsthand experience.

The danger lies in how these assumptions can guide our interactions, coloring our perceptions, and distorting the reality of individuals' behavior or intentions within the larger cultural picture. Hence, their propensity to mold our responses can escalate a harmless or unintentional act into a larger conflict or misunderstanding.

9.3. Assumptions and Miscommunication

Now that we understand how assumptions form and their impact on our cross-cultural interactions, let's delve deeper into how they contribute to miscommunication. Miscommunication can surface in numerous forms - misinterpreted signals, taken-for-granted use of language, and conflicts arising from contrasting cultural norms and values.

Between cultures, non-verbal cues can be as illuminating as they are misleading. The same gesture might bear different meanings in different cultures - a nod could equal agreement or simply an acknowledgement in different parts of the world. Oftentimes, we attribute the meaning we are accustomed to, regardless of its cultural context, thus sparking the potential for misunderstanding.

Language poses another domain of complexity. With words and phrases steeped in cultural context, interpretations can be clouded by the naivety or ignorance of an alien culture. All these missteps, while innocently intended, can potentially pave the way for conflicts, stress, and strained relationships.

9.4. Navigating the Minefield: Strategies to Counter Assumptions

Developing awareness and strategies to counter assumptions is a critical first step towards effective intercultural communication. Some of these strategies may include:

1. Cultivating Cultural Awareness: Cultivating an awareness of other cultures and their unique aspects can be enlightening. It can provide a deeper understanding of cultural nuances, minimizing stereotypes and preconceptions.

2. Developing Empathy: Empathy is the bedrock of any meaningful relationship. In the context of intercultural communication, empathy involves the capacity to view the world from another person's perspective, reducing the inclination to make hasty assumptions.

3. Fostering Open-mindedness: Adopting an open-minded approach towards understanding and respecting different cultures can ease the road to intercultural communication. The embrace of diversity can mitigate preconceived notions and create an environment conducive to engagement and learning.

4. Encourage Feedback: Encourage continuous feedback in your communication, to ensure clarity and mutual understanding, mitigate misinterpretations, and cater to adaptability and growth.

In conclusion, assumptions form an invisible but significant barrier in intercultural communication that can swiftly escalate into conflict and misunderstanding. By developing cultural awareness, empathy, and openness, as well as fostering continuous feedback, we can dismantle these barriers and foster effective and respectful intercultural communication.

Chapter 10. The Essentials of Intercultural Adaptation

Cultural adaptation begins when we step outside our comfort zone, outside the familiar landscapes of our routine life. It is something we face when we travel to a new place, interact with people from different cultural backgrounds, or simply when we are exposed to an unfamiliar cultural context. The process of cultural adaptation can be challenging, at times creating a feeling of disorientation, but it is essential to effective intercultural communication.

10.1. Understanding Cultural Differences

Different cultures around the world have unique traditions, customs, values and ways of expressing thoughts and emotions. Cultural differences can be subtle or blatant, complex or straightforward. These differences are manifested in various ways such as language, etiquette, non-verbal communication, norms and values, or even our concept of time and space. These factors can shape our perspective, control our reactions, and dictate our behavior.

For instance, in many Asian cultures, too much direct eye contact might be considered disrespectful, whereas in Western cultures it's seen as a sign of honesty and engagement. Similarly, gestures that are acceptable in one culture might be offensive in another. The 'OK' sign, made by connecting the thumb and forefinger in a circle, is positive in English-speaking countries but offensive or vulgar in some other parts of the world.

10.2. Adapting to New Cultural Environments

Adapting to a new culture is not just about learning and adapting to the visible elements like food, language, and clothing. It's about understanding the underlying values, attitudes, and beliefs that motivate people's behavior and actions.

It's crucial to be open-minded, observant, and flexible while adapting to a new cultural environment. Ask questions, listen actively, watch local habits and customs, and try to understand the cultural logic behind these behaviors. Moreover, being sensitive, respectful, and patient towards cultural nuances can facilitate your adaptation process and foster meaningful relationships.

10.3. Elements of Cultural Adaptation

In order to adapt effectively to new cultures, we need to consider a few elements that will aid in this transition:

- The Language: Learning the language is one of the most concrete ways you can get closer to a new culture. Language is a window into the psyche of a culture, and it can give important insights into how people think, how they express their thoughts and emotions, and how they perceive the world.

- Cultural Norms and Values: Every culture has its own set of rules that regulates social behavior. Learning these cultural norms and values not only helps in managing day-to-day interactions, but it also provides an understanding of the acceptable and unacceptable behaviors within that culture.

- Social Structure: Understanding the structure of social relationships within the culture helps to navigate social situations smoothly. This might include understanding gender roles, familial structures, class dynamics, and more.

- Communication Style: Every culture has a particular communication style that needs to be understood. This includes both verbal (language style, tone, conversation rules) and non-verbal cues (gestures, facial expressions, body language).

10.4. Overcoming Cultural Shock

Cultural shock is a common consequence of diving into a new culture. Feelings of confusion, disorientation, or even anxiety when encountering unfamiliar cultural practices are normal. Overcoming this requires patience, resilience, and a positive attitude. Following are the strategies to deal with culture shock:

- Learning about the Culture: Research and read about the destination culture. This will help prepare mentally for the new environment.

- Support Network: Build a support network. This could include locals, fellow expats, or even a counselor who is experienced in intercultural adaptation.

- Maintain Familiar Routines: Keeping a bit of familiarity in daily life while adapting to new routines helps to alleviate feelings of disorientation.

- Cultural Empathy: Develop empathy for the host culture and try to see things from this new perspective.

- Healthy Lifestyle: Regular exercise, a healthy diet and enough sleep can do wonders in maintaining emotional balance under culturally shocking situations.

Understanding and adapting to cultural differences doesn't happen overnight. It's a journey that requires patience, curiosity, respect, and empathy. Remember that differences are not deficiencies, but opportunities to learn, grow and connect deeply with others. As the adage goes, "When in Rome, do as the Romans do." With this approach, let's unlock the secrets of mastering cultural adaptation in intercultural communication.

Chapter 11. Looking Forward: The Evolving Landscape of Intercultural Communication

Our age is often characterized as a time of swift and continuous change, and it seems clear that the face of intercultural communication will keep evolving along the same pace. Globalization and technological advancements not only bring about economic transformations but have also reshaped our understanding of culture and communication in the process. We are connected, now more than ever, as vast networks of information link us together, making distances feel shorter and differences feel less significant. But the question remains: what is the future landscape of intercultural communication? How is it evolving? And what will be our role?

11.1. Globalization and its Impacts on Communication

Globalization has worked to intensify international and intercultural relations. The continuous enlargement of international trade, the proliferation of multinational corporations, and the ease of travel have brought cultures closer to one another. This interaction has led to inevitable exchanges, fusions, and conflicts that have driven the evolution of intercultural communication. As the world becomes more complex, so does our need to understand cultures and communicate effectively.

Moreover, globalization has compelling implications for languages. English has emerged as a lingua franca in many global contexts, but the heightened interface among cultures has also led to revitalizing, preserving and even creating languages. This is a key phenomenon in navigating the evolving landscape of intercultural communication as language shapes our thoughts and how we perceive the world.

11.2. Digital Revolution: Bridging Cultures or Dividing Them?

The digital revolution, characterized by the explosion of social media, has altered how we relate to and understand other cultures. It has provided platforms for instantaneous communication, opened up spaces for diverse voices, and blurred geographical boundaries. However, it has also facilitated the formation of echo chambers and spread of misinformation, leading to miscommunication or exacerbating cultural divides.

Moreover, as Artificial Intelligence (AI) continues to evolve, its strong potential in breaking down language barriers through real-time translation services is undeniable. At the same time, the dialectic nature of technological advancements also poses questions about its potential risks. Consider the challenges of machine learning in understanding and respecting cultural nuances or the risk of losing languages and associated cultural richness under the dominance of certain languages supported by such technologies.

11.3. Education for Intercultural Competency: The Key Influence

As the global landscape continues to morph, the importance of education in shaping attitudes towards other cultures cannot be overstated. Beyond language proficiency, cultural competence that comprises knowledge, attitudes, skills, and behavior is becoming increasingly crucial for effective communication. Multicultural education and diversity training can promote understanding, respect, and appreciation of cultural differences, thus enhancing communication.

Programs fostering youth exchange, study abroad, cross-cultural training, and virtual collaborations are also gaining prominence. These tools not only build cultural competency from an early age, but they also offer first-hand experience of different cultures, fostering empathy and understanding.

11.4. Anticipating Cultural Shifts: An Ongoing Challenge

Recognizing that culture is dynamic and ever-changing is vital in predicting the evolving landscape of intercultural communication. Cultural shifts, driven by changing values, population mobility, or social transformations, fundamentally alter the way cultures interact and communicate. Therefore, staying attuned to these shifts is integral for businesses, policymakers, educators, and everyone in between to communicate effectively in an increasingly globalized world.

11.5. Charting the Course for the Future

Given these trends, it is evident intercultural communication will continue to evolve at an accelerated pace. The power of effective communication in a diverse, interconnected world is tremendous and yet, it requires continuous learning, understanding, and adaptation.

As we step into the future, we should keep our minds open and cultivate a willingness to learn about and from different cultures. While the landscape of intercultural communication can be intricate and challenging, it is also immensely rewarding. Embracing intercultural communication in its full capacity will help us not just to interact, but to understand and empathize with each other on a global scale. Proceed then, with both optimism and caution, as we navigate the evolving dynamics of intercultural communication.

www.ingramcontent.com/pod-product-compliance
Lightning Source LLC
Chambersburg PA
CBHW062306290526
45794CB00006B/2709